preface

William Twining

The problems of public order in an emergency pose agonising choices and stir deep passions. The subject is topical and urgent in Northern Ireland to-day, but it has a much wider significance, for it raises basic questions about any society's response to dissent and to violence. It is not just a problem in Ulster: it is also a British problem, an Irish problem and a world problem. This study is intended to contribute constructively to reasoned and informed public debate on one aspect of the matter: that is: what would constitute a satisfactory legislative framework of powers and safeguards to be invoked in situations where public order or internal security is seriously threatened?

The answer outlined here is presented as a starting point for discussion rather than as a blue-print. It was worked out by members of an informal and entirely unofficial group of law students and law teachers at the Queen's University, Belfast during the academic year 1971-72. Our varied backgrounds and our immediate context influenced our approach in a number of ways: living and working in Northern Ireland we were daily reminded of the immediacy and the human realities of the problems we were discussing; professional concerns led us to concentrate on the technical and practical aspects; several of us were able to draw on the experience of other jurisdictions; the atmosphere of Queen's reminded us of the value of striving for relative detachment even on the most emotive topics; as individuals of quite varied political persuasions we were searching for common ground in the belief that this is an area where widespread consent and consensus in respect of principle are of the essence: if they are lacking any attempted solution is, in the long run, almost bound to fail. An encouraging feature of this exercise was that we were able to reach agreement on principles and to sink our differences on points of detail.

A tentative draft of this pamphlet was circulated privately in March 1972 to a number of people in public life in Northern Ireland, Britain and the Republic of Ireland. Some revisions were made in the light of comments received, and a final draft was later agreed. Having completed its task, the group dissolved. Apart from minor editorial corrections the text has remained unchanged. There have been many relevant events in Northern Ireland since then, but nothing has happened which, in my view, invalidates the main arguments and suggestions presented here. There is still a need for an alternative to internment; there is more than ever a need for effective methods of preventing and dealing with grievances arising out of the actions of the security forces; the replacement of the out dated and unpopular legislation, which has, inter alia, acquired a great symbolic significance, is overdue. There is, in short, a more urgent need than ever for a fresh start.

September 1972.

1. introduction

This pamphlet is concerned with the future. It sets out proposals for a new Emergency Powers (Security) Act based on principles which, it is hoped, will be acceptable to reasonable thinking people of widely differing viewpoints. The occasion for making these recommendations is the present situation in Northern Ireland. The problems of a divided community, the historical background to the present crisis and experience of the operation of the Civil Authorities (Special Powers) Act, 1922 (the Special Powers Act) and cognate legislation have all been in the forefront. But the legislative framework that is recommended here could be equally suitable for implementation anywhere in the British Isles. Some of the technical details might vary, but the underlying principles and standards should be the same.

It is a mark of a civilised society that certain standards of behaviour and restraint should be observed by all parties to a dispute and that those in authority, as guardians of the community's values, have a special duty to set an example in upholding such standards even under great provocation and stress. As Lord MacDermott said, in speaking of the long tradition of resistance to arbitrary rule and oppression in the British Isles, at the University of Dundee in December 1971: " It has to be protected for the way of life it enshrines, but . . . the protection cannot be allowed to choke or cramp the essence of what is protected " (*Juridical Review,* April 1972, p 1). It is from this starting point then that the difficult topic of emergency powers is approached—that is to say the question of the extent, the manner of the exercise and the safeguards against abuse of extraordinary powers granted to a government when the public order or the security of the state is seriously threatened.

limitations of proposals

Clearly there are severe limits to what can be achieved by legislation alone. It would be absurd to suggest that a new Emergency Powers (Security) Act will strike at the root of " the Irish question." It is equally absurd to suggest that the mere fact of decreeing a set of formal rules and procedures will guarantee that arbitrariness and abuse of power will be eliminated or that the rules will never be exceeded or infringed. But there are both symbolic and practical reasons why the subject is an important one in the present context. First, the Special Powers Act has become a potent symbol of repression in the eyes of one section of the community in Northern Ireland. At the same time, calls for the repeal of the Special Powers Act show a lack of realism if they impliedly suggest that there should be no legislative provision at all for emergency powers. A new Emergency Powers (Security) Act, marking a fresh start, which clearly embodies values common to the various sections of the community and which is in accordance with the standards accepted as civilized by the world community, could serve the function of reasserting these values. Secondly, at a more down to earth level, recent events have exposed many defects, loopholes and inconsistencies in the law dealing with emergency powers. It gives inadequate guidance to the security forces, to the citizen and to the courts, it is silent on many matters and it draws not at all on the recent experience of other jurisdictions in dealing with the problems of internal security. It is crude, primitive and outdated. Thus, quite apart from political considerations, there are good practical reasons for asserting that a fresh start is overdue.

the problem

Under " normal " conditions in peace time in most countries certain basic assumptions about the scope and limitations and legitimacy of governmental power are not challenged by the vast majority of members of the community. Many citizens may oppose or dislike the current rulers, yet recognise that they constitute the legitimate government. They may disagree with the details of particular provisions relating to the maintenance of order, the preservation of the security of the state, and the control of crime, but they accept that some powers to secure these objectives are necessary and justified. But they may also assume that a mark of civilized society is that there must be strict limits to the scope of such powers and there must be standards with regard to the manner of their exercise. Such limitations on and standards for the exercise of power by governments are often referred to generically by the emotive, but ill-defined, phrase " the rule of law." Historically the inhabitants of the various jurisdictions of the British Isles have placed great emphasis on values associated with the rule of law, for example, freedom from arbitrary search and arrest, the right to a fair trial, protection from unfair methods of interrogation, and effective legal remedies against unlawful actions by the authorities.

Serious problems arise when some of these assumptions are challenged—when, for instance, a substantial proportion of the population questions the legitimacy of the regime in power or where the ordinary powers and techniques available to government seem to be inadequate to deal with some challenge to public order. Both these conditions are claimed to exist in Northern Ireland, with representatives of different factions laying more stress on one than on the other. In such conditions not only do the tensions between the rule of law and the maintenance of public order and security become acute, but also many people find it difficult to separate their attitude to the regime from their attitude to the means it uses to maintain order. Thus much of the public debate on various forms of violence that have been used recently has involved the application of a double standard: when *they* use violence it is evil; when *we* use it, it is in a righteous cause. But it is both possible and desirable to distinguish questions about the scope of emergency powers from questions about the legitimacy or acceptability of the regime that will exercise such powers. Thus, in making recommendations for an Emergency Powers (Security) Act, we must assume the legitimacy of the legislature which enacts it, without necessarily committing ourselves to who that legislature should be. In short, there are standards which any government should observe. To draw a distinction between questions about *who* governs and questions about *how* they should govern, does not make the question of legitimacy irrelevant. For instance, it is a good reason for a government to use restraint in exercising its lawful powers, if the implementation of such powers may have the effect of alienating a section of the community. One of the most cogent arguments against internment in Northern Ireland is that it may have contributed to the alienation from the existing regime of a section of the community and thus increased their support for the IRA. Whether this has in fact happened and, if so, to what extent is one of the differences of fact between supporters and opponents of internment.

what is an emergency?

The situation in Northern Ireland also raises the question what is an emergency. In many jurisdictions a sharp distinction is drawn between " normal times " and " a state of emergency." In normal times the powers of government in respect of security are strictly limited by the constitution and the law of the land. Normal times can probably only be defined in negative terms. Times are normal when a state is not at war and when there is no public emergency threatening the life of the nation. This formulation is recognised by Article 15 of the European Convention for the Protection of Human Rights and Fundamental Freedoms, which states: " In time of war or other public emergency threatening the life of the nation any High Contracting Party may take measures derogating from its obligations under this convention to the extent strictly required by the exigencies of the situation, provided that such measures are not inconsistent with its other obligations under international law." Before special or extraordinary powers can be invoked a state of emergency has to be declared by the duly authorised body, often according to some prescribed procedure. Sometimes a State of Emergency can be declared indefinitely, sometimes it can only last for a limited period, subject to renewal. There is considerable variety even among common law jurisdictions as to the conditions under which an emergency may be declared, who may declare it, and the powers that are granted in such circumstances, but the most common pattern is to give to the Executive the power of proclaiming a state of emergency for a limited period, but to provide for some form of legislative control. For instance, in Britain the Emergency Powers Act, 1920 (as amended by the Emergency Powers Act, 1964), which deals with emergencies arising out of threats to essential supplies and services, provides that Her Majesty may declare a state of emergency for not more than one month, but that Parliament, if not in session, must be summoned by a proclamation to be issued within five days of the declaration of the emergency and regulations made under the proclamation of emergency must be laid before Parliament as soon as possible.

In contrast, the Special Powers Act contains neither a requirement of a declaration of a State of Emergency nor a provision automatically invalidating regulations which have not been approved by the Houses of Parliament though regulations may be annulled by the Governor on the prayer of one of the Houses if made within 14 days of the regulation being laid. In a sense Northern Ireland is treated as being in a permanent state of emergency. The Emergency Powers Act (NI), 1926, which corresponds to the English Act of 1920, contains no time limit on the duration of an emergency, and although regulations must be laid before Parliament there is no requirement either of affirmation of the declaration of emergency or of the regulations ; nor is there any provision for annulment of such regulations on the resolution of Parliament.

2. the special powers act

The Civil Authorities (Special Powers) Act received the Royal Assent on 7 April 1922. According to its preamble it was " An Act to empower certain authorities of the Government of Northern Ireland to take steps for preserving the peace and maintaining order in Northern Ireland, and for purposes connected therewith." The act was necessitated by a decision of the British Cabinet at the end of January 1922 after agreement with the Southern Irish leaders had been reached. The United Kingdom Government was not, in view of this political settlement, prepared to allow the Restoration of Order in Ireland Act 1920 to be enforced in any part of Ireland. The Prime Minister of Northern Ireland, Sir James Craig, was to be informed that he should make his own legislative arrangements to deal with the situation and that if military force was necessary this should for the future be used under common law powers and the King's Regulations (CAB 24, 132). Continuing armed violence both within and across the border of Northern Ireland made it seem imperative to the authorities that such legislation be enacted.

In 1920 in order to authorise the use of wartime powers the Restoration of Order in Ireland Act had empowered the making of regulations under the Defence of the Realm Consolidation Act 1914, under which power to make regulations had only been conferred for the period of the War which had begun in 1914. The Civil Authorities (Special Powers) Act 1922 differed from the Restoration of Order in Ireland Act 1920 in that it makes no reference to courts martial, the latter Act authorising the trial of all persons who had committed crimes in Ireland to take place by court martial. In other respects the Acts showed marked similarity. For example, the regulation making powers were similar and the original thirty regulations made as a schedule to the 1922 Act were all directly adopted from the Restoration of Order in Ireland Act Regulations (NIHC *Debates,* vol II, col 90-91).

The result of the Civil Authorities (Special Powers) Act and Regulations, when taken in conjunction with the existence of the special constabulary, was that, apart from the fact that no military courts existed, the Government was able to exercise powers of more or less the same amplitude as those available to it in time of martial law. Indeed at the end of May 1922 it was suggested at a British Cabinet meeting that martial law be formally introduced in Northern Ireland, but the suggestion was rejected on the grounds that not only would such a step be taken as indicating lack of confidence to the Northern Ireland Government, but also because, apart from the use of courts martial, martial law powers were in effect being exercised (CAB 23, 30 May 1922).

Following the pattern of temporary duration set by the Defence of the Realm Consolidation Act 1920 the Civil Authorities (Special Powers) Act was to remain in force for one year. The Special Powers Act (the colloquial description of the Act) was renewed annually from 1923 to 1927. In 1928 the Parliament of Northern Ireland continued the Act in force for a period of five years. In 1933 a further Act provided that the 1922 Act should continue in force until Parliament otherwise determined. There have subsequently been minor amendments to the Act, but, in view of the likelihood of recurring violence, there has been no alteration in the general nature and scope of the powers it has conferred and their indefinite duration.

the rule making power

Section one of the Special Powers Act confers two powers for preserving peace and maintaining order, which, according to the decision of the House of Lords in *McEldowney v Forde* (1971, AC, 632) are separate and distinct.

First, subsection one gives the " civil authority " power " to take all such steps and issue all such orders as may be necessary for preserving the peace and maintaining order." The " civil authority " is, by subsection two, the Minister of Home Affairs, but he may delegate this power either to his Parliamentary Secretary or to an officer of the Royal Ulster Constabulary (in practice the Chief Constable). According to *McEldowney v Forde* this power is a purely administrative one. It is however subject to a proviso: "Provided that the ordinary course of law and avocations of life and the enjoyment of property shall be interfered with as little as may be permitted by the exigencies of the steps required to be taken under this Act." The meaning of this proviso is not easy to understand, unless it serves to emphasise the requirement to act only "as may be necessary." The decision in *O'Hanlon* (1922, 56 ILTR, 170), which was an early attempt to impugn the power of internment under the Act, serves to illustrate this. The Court was satisfied that the Act and the relevant regulation and order were within the competence of the Parliament of Northern Ireland and the Minister respectively. Their jurisdiction went no further. If the courts adopt a similar attitude in evaluating the necessity of executive action to that taken in construing legislative action by the Minister, then if the action is normally within the competence of the Minister, there seems to be little chance of judicial review.

The other power conferred on the Minister is legislative and is conferred by subsection three. He is given power to make regulations "for making further provision for the preservation of the peace and maintenance of order" and for varying or revoking any provision of the regulations already in existence. By subsection four a regulation must be laid before both Houses of Parliament. It *may* be annulled by the Governor (acting of course on the advice of the executive) if an address praying annulment is presented to him by either House within fourteen days of the regulation being laid before it. Parliament can of course at any time repeal or amend the section or any other part of the Act.

content of the act

The Special Powers Act contains 10 main sections and numerous regulations. We have already examined section 1 above. The other sections make provision for offences against the regulations (including as an offence any act prejudicial to the preservation of peace and not specifically provided for in the regulations); for the trial of offences to be instituted by the Attorney-General and to be before two resident magistrates; for the punishment of offences (including allowing the death penalty in certain explosives cases); for the power of arrest; for the taking of depositions in certain cases; for the prohibition of inquests in certain circumstances; and lastly for compensation for damage to property.

The regulations are very varied in their scope. Powers to search, stop and seize motor vehicles, arrest, and to disperse a crowd of three or more people are all exercisable on suspicion by the person given the powers (usually any member of the police force or the armed forces). The Civil Authority has power to block roads, impose a curfew, control all road vehicles, and take over property and erect buildings and structures. The Minister of Home Affairs has power to censor under the new general provision which took effect last year. The Chief Constable of the RUC has power to control railway traffic. The Civil Authority has, in addition, a complete right of access to all property, and power to seize money or property which he has reason to suspect has been collected for a purpose prejudicial to peace or order. Any officer of the RUC may order the detention for questioning of any person for up to 48 hours (the person can then be released and detained for a further 48 hours). The power to intern is vested in the Minister of Home Affairs, acting on the advice of a senior police officer or advisory committee. The Minister may also make an application to a court asking that the public be excluded from a trial, and the court may, but is not obliged to, order the exclusion of the public. Duties are placed on the public to stop and answer to the best of one's ability, when so required by a member of the police force or the armed forces. A person coming into Northern Ireland may be required to satisfy the authority that his presence will not be prejudicial to peace or order in Northern Ireland. The following are included among the offences against the regulations: possession of an offensive weapon, causing injury to roads or railways, membership of an unlawful organisation, wire-tapping, possession of a code or cipher, possession of information about the police which might be useful to an enemy, claiming to act under a permit when not so authorised, and endangering the safety of a person acting in the execution of a duty given him by the Civil Authority.

operational history

During the years 1922 and 1923 the powers under the Act were widely used. Internment was brought in to try to cope with the "troubles". During this period some regulations were added to those included in the original Schedule. When the "troubles" died down the use of the powers was reduced and regulation making also ceased. Internment however continued until 1926 (NIHC *Debates,* vol VL, col 1969).

The period of 1931-36 was a time of intense political activity North and South. Of the four new regulations made in this period, three were concerned with banning political parties. The Minister exercised his other powers frequently during this period. Internment was again introduced around Christmas 1938 (NIHC *Debates,* vol XXII, col 415). From the end of the war until 1954, many of the provisions of the Act were not actively invoked. Many regulations were revoked in the period 1949-51, and few prosecutions were brought under the Act although in 1950 outbreaks of isolated violence led to internment being introduced for a time. (A survey of the years 1945-55 showed that there were no prosecutions in the years 1945-49; 1951-53; 1955 and comparatively few in the other years: Edwards, "Special powers in Northern Ireland," 1956, *Criminal Law Review,* 7.) It is interesting to note when considering this period that in 1954 when eight men were arrested after an attack on Omagh military barracks they were successfully prosecuted not under the Special Powers Act but under the ordinary criminal law. In 1952 the Minister successfully banned an Orange Parade for the first time. From 1954 onwards many of the powers given under the regulations which had been revoked in 1949 and 1951 were reintroduced in new form. The regulations of 1954-55 were mainly entry and search powers, and one regulation banned a new splinter group of the Republican movement. After the IRA campaign was launched on 12 December 1956, a large number of regulations was made. These re-activated internment, detention, censorship, curfew, special trial procedures, the firearms control regulations, and banned two more political organisations. Regulations concerning movement restriction, arrest and control of explosives were made in 1957. It is these regulations made between 1954 and 1957 which form the bulk of the present schedule of the Special Powers Act. These regulations were supplemented in 1966 by three more. The first concerned the power to stop and search trains, the second two arose because of militant activity which had resulted in the formation of the Protestant Ulster Volunteer Force (UVF) and in a number of murders. The UVF was banned and an assembly of more than two persons was made illegal. The following year the Minister of Home Affairs banned Republican Clubs "or any like organisation howsoever described" because he said they were being formed to circumvent the ban imposed on Sinn Fein in 1956.

The most recent phase of regulation making began in 1969 following the rioting of July, August and September of that year. Three regulations were made giving power to regulate firearms, entertainment and licensed premises. The two 1970 regulations enabled the Minister to impose a blanket ban on marches and processions, and increased the powers of the military to disperse a crowd of three or more persons. Several regulations were made in 1971. They imposed a duty to inform the authorities of any death or wounding caused by an offensive weapon or explosives, enabled the Minister to regulate funerals, and made it an offence to prejudice the preservation of peace by dressing or behaving as though a member of a quasi-military organisation. Another replaced the old censorship provision (regulation 8), which had been used since 1954 to ban Republican papers, by a more general provision. Prosecutions under the censorship regulations seem at all times to have been rare, but a prosecution was recently brought, apparently for possessing " documents relating to the affairs of the IRA " against a person who had in his house two newspapers—*Republican News* and *An Phoblact.* Another regulation made additions to the internment regulations. Internment was re-activated by the Prime Minister acting as Minister of Home Affairs on 9 August 1971.

criticisms

There has been widespread criticism of the Special Powers Act since 1922 when the Act was passed. We feel it is important to examine these criticisms without necessarily accepting their validity mainly because any attempt to make proposals or to legislate without taking into account the areas of discontent that have arisen previously may allow such discontents to arise again. We have not tried to be comprehensive but merely to examine the areas of criticism which we think are the most important.

1. The Special Powers Act is criticised because of the width of the powers which have been given and the lack of any satisfactory control over the exercise of those powers either by the courts or by Parliament. Thus, as we have seen above, the Minister of Home Affairs is given power to make regulations " for making further provision for the preservation of the peace and the maintenance of order " and for varying or revoking any provision of the regulation already in existence. The width of such a power makes many regulations practically uncontestable in the courts. Thus, for example, in *McEldowney v Forde* (1971, AC, 632) the House of Lords by a majority held a regulation which banned " Republican clubs or any like organisation howsoever described " to be valid since it could have the effect of controlling subversive activity, even though the regulation was so vague that it made criminal a great deal of completely innocuous conduct. Another extremely wide provision is Section 2(4) which provides: " If any person does any act of such a nature as to be calculated to be prejudicial to the preservation of the peace or maintenance of order in Northern Ireland and not specifically provided for in the regulations he shall be deemed to be guilty of an offence against the regulations."

This seems to be a clear breach of the doctrine *nulla poena sine lege,* now embodied in Article 11(2) of the Universal Declaration of Human Rights and Fundamental Freedoms 1948. This provides that "No restrictions shall be placed on the exercise of these rights other than such as are prescribed by law and are necessary in a democratic society in the interests of national security or public safety, for the prevention of disorder or crime, for the protection of health or morals or for the protection of the rights and freedoms of others . . ."

2. It is also alleged that the discretion given to the Minister of Home Affairs under the Act has been abused. Allegations of lack of impartiality are often made. Such allegations are reinforced by Professor N. Mansergh's assertion that the Government of Northern Ireland " was unduly subservient to the Orange Order in a guarantee publicly given that the provisions of the Civil Authorities Act should not be used against any of its members " (*Government of Northern Ireland,* p 246) Thus the Government's attitude to certain marches has been seen to be due to this, notably the revocation of the ban on the 1935 " Twelfth " Orange Parade after the Orange Grand Master said he would defy such a ban (*Report to Westminster MPs on the 1935 riots*). It has been said that this Parade was a direct cause of the serious rioting which ensued (*Report of the advisory committee on Police in Northern Ireland,* Cmd 535, para. 24). The failure of the Government to ban the Apprentice Boys Parade in Derry on 12 August 1969 has also been alleged to have been due to lack of impartiality. In the opinion of the Scarman Tribunal the decision not to ban the march was justified in the light of all the

evidence available to the Minister of Home Affairs at the time (*Report of a tribunal of inquiry into Violence and Civil Disturbances in Northern Ireland in 1969,* Cmd 566, April 1972). Similarly the fact that the Ministerial discretion was used to ban the 1970 March by the Apprentice Boys under the Special Powers Act and not as previously under the Public Order Act is seen by critics of the Government as a decision taken to ensure that the supporters of the Government who broke the ban would not be subject to the mandatory prison sentence of six months (K. Boyle, "Minimum Sentences Act," *Northern Ireland Legal Quarterly,* 1970). This would have been the case if the ban had been imposed under the Public Order Acts because by virtue of the Criminal Justice (Temporary Provisions) Act (NI) 1970 a six month prison sentence for breaking a ban on marches imposed under the Public Order Act was made mandatory. Those concerned in these decisions have pointed out that it would not in the view of the Ministry's advisers have been legal to impose a ban on these processions under the Public Order Act in view of the fact that the reason for imposing the ban was that it would impose an undue burden on the security forces rather than that there was an immediate threat to public order. The Minister's power has also been used, it is alleged, to suppress not only political activity which was against the present constitutional position of Northern Ireland, but also political activity directed towards an amelioration of economic circumstances (NCCL, *Report on the Special Powers Act,* 1936). Examples of this that have been given include the fact that in 1925 the unemployed of Belfast were banned from marching on the same day as the opening of the Northern Ireland Parliament because the Minister said that it was an attempt to intimidate the Government (Andrew Boyd, *The rise of the Irish Trade Unions 1729-1970,* p 99, 1972); that in 1932 the Out-door Relief Workers were banned from demonstrating (*ibid,* p 103) and that the Act was also used during the Second World War against industrial strikers.

3. The allegation is made that certain powers given in the Regulations are ultra vires the Government of Ireland Act 1920. This argument was upheld to a limited extent in *R v Justices of the Peace for the County of the City of Londonderry ex parte Hume et al* (23 February 1972) where it was decided that the Northern Ireland Parliament had not the power to give the Minister of Home Affairs power to authorise the armed forces to act under certain regulations since laws "in respect of" the army, navy or air force are excepted matters by virtue of the Government of Ireland Act 1920.

4. Many of the allegations and criticisms concern the use of the controversial powers of detention and internment without trial. These powers are alleged to have been used almost entirely against one section of the community to an extent not strictly required by the exigencies of the situation but again as a means of suppressing political opposition. Internment has also been criticised as leading to a contempt for the judicial processes by its use against people immediately after they have been acquitted of criminal charges, or in rearresting those whose release has been ordered by the courts on the ground of some irregularity in the original arrest and detention (T. Hadden, "The Rule of Law in Northern Ireland," *New Law Journal,* 17 February, 1972, p 161). There have also been allegations that the threat of internment has been used to secure the compliance of people with the wishes of the security forces. For example it was alleged in *Moore v Minister of Home Affairs* in Amagh County Court, February 1972, that the threat of internment was used to deter the prosecution of a civil action against the authorities. Other specific criticisms relate to the lack of adequate safeguards concerning the use of internment. The following defects especially have been criticised (C. Palley, *The Times,* 23 November 1971):

(a) The lack of constant supervision by Parliament.

(b) The lack of a rapid procedure for Parliament to end internment by resolution.

(c) The inability of the committee under

Judge Brown to make decisions which are binding on the executive.

(d) The inability of persons detained, but not interned to apply for release to the Advisory Committee under Judge Brown.

(e) The difficulty of finding out where persons held for interrogation are being kept.

(f) The lack of adequate compensation.

3. theoretical considerations

In proposing a replacement for the Special Powers Act we are suggesting that there are civilized limits and standards for the exercise of power by government, when public order and the security of the state are threatened from within. At the outset a sceptic may ask: "What possible basis can there be for such standards? Is this not a matter of subjective preference?" This is a fair question and one which admits of no easy answer. For example, in recent debates on internment arguments both for and against it appear to have been based on quite varied assumptions. At least four types of argument are regularly advanced.

First, there are those who appear to maintain an absolute ethical position, sometimes based on natural law or natural rights, sometimes on bare assertion. Such arguments take the form that "detention or internment without trial by any regime is justified under no circumstances, without exception" or "the state is entitled to use any means whatsoever to protect itself from a ruthless enemy." It has been our experience that some people who assert such positions are prepared, at least in private, to concede that they would have to admit to exceptions to such propositions. Thus it is possible to start from what looks like absolutist positions on internment and cognate matters, and to accept after argument that in the general area of emergency powers the problem often boils down to a choice between two evils in respect of which it is difficult to maintain that one of the evils is absolute, but the other is not. Even where someone insists, after discussion, that he would rule out certain kinds of methods of maintaining order in all circumstances without exception, it is for him to clarify the *scope* of the means he believes to be unjustifiable. And exploration of this question may reveal that in practice the difference between an absolute ethical position and that of an ethical relativist or utilitarian may not be very great.

Another basis for "civilized standards" which is commonly invoked is the fact of the international acceptance of certain standards of civilized government. Such standards are, for instance, to be found in documents such as the Universal Declaration of Human Rights, 1948 and the European Convention for the Protection of Human Rights and Fundamental Freedoms, 1950. Invocation of the European Convention, where applicable, is an especially persuasive argument in the British Isles, for both the governments of the United Kingdom and the Republic of Ireland are signatories to the Convention. This means that not only are they bound by international law to observe its provisions, but also they have publicly accepted the Convention as laying down firm minimum standards of civilized behaviour which they undertake to observe. We believe that the standards set by the Convention do in fact reflect a broad consensus in world public opinion and informed opinion in the British Isles and for this reason provide a relatively firm basis for proposals about emergency powers. Accordingly we propose that an Emergency Powers (Security) Act should not only be consistent with, but should also reflect the underlying approach of the relevant provisions of the European Convention.

A third type of argument involves an historical appeal to the traditions of the British and the Irish who have always been freedom loving peoples, and have set an example to the world in resisting oppression and arbitrary government. Any provision for the protection of public security and order must be consistent with the spirit of these traditions. This argument has a strong emotional appeal to many and it serves as a useful reminder of some of the most important values which have provided the basis for government in our societies in the past. If sufficient people are prepared to reaffirm these values, then it holds out some hope for consensus in the future. However, the fact must be faced that the traditions and values that are thus invoked are open to a variety of interpretations and that they are too general to provide precise guidance in determining the line to be drawn between legitimate governmental power and unacceptable breaches of the rule of law.

A fourth type of argument which is commonly used in discussing emergency powers is a utilitarian argument. Such arguments purport to assess the acceptability of a particular measure by reference to whether its consequences are likely in fact to increase or decrease the sum total of human happiness. As we shall see, it is possible to invoke such arguments in support of and against the introduction of internment on 9 August 1971. For instance, advocates of internment maintain that it is both a necessary and efficient means of combating the IRA and that the pain involved in the detention without trial of persons suspected of terrorism is outweighed by the lives and property that have been saved by this means. On the other hand, some critics of internment maintain that it has been counter productive, in that it has led to an increase of violence and has alienated the minority community.

common ground

Disagreement between people invoking utilitarian arguments are often reducible to questions of fact. This seems to be the case in the present debate about internment. For instance, some common ground may be found between many supporters and opponents of internment in the present situation in respect of the following formulation:

1. Internment without trial is an evil which is justified if and only if certain conditions are satisfied;

2. Deprivation of liberty is an evil but from the point of view of those who consider the existing order legitimate, threats to the security of the state or the disruption of normal life through violence or certain other kinds of activity are worse evils. Deprivation of liberty to the minimum extent necessary and with as few additional discomforts as possible may be justified, provided that this is the only feasible means of achieving the desired security; *and* it is likely in fact to further this; *and* it is not likely to have secondary effects which are worse than the evil to be prevented; *and* adequate safeguards are provided to ensure that the selection and the treatment of detainees does not step beyond the bounds of the justification for their detention; *and* effective remedies are available against illegal acts committed in implementing a policy of internment.

We believe that some such general formulation as this would be acceptable to many people who nonetheless disagree as to whether or not the decision of 9 August was justified. What then is the basis for their disagreement? One common reason is that many people who have taken stands on internment have just not thought the problem through. For them this kind of analysis may be helpful and may reduce disagreement. A second ground for difference of opinion is over the evaluation of the good and evil involved. Some may sincerely believe that detention without trial is an unmitigated evil. Others may seek to balance the weight to be attached to loss of liberty for a period against the risk of death or injury to citizens going about their business. Some disagreement may be eliminated by clarification of the nature and extent of the phenomena being evaluated, but ultimately the matter rests on subjective value judgments. Thirdly, people with similar values may disagree about what the consequences are in fact or are likely to be. For instance some maintain that the IRA has in fact been strengthened because of internment by gaining sympathy and by the effects of internment on the internees themselves. Others maintain that internment has severely weakened the IRA and that its alienating effect is likely to be only temporary. Each side may produce elaborate statistics about the incidence of violence and the success of the security operation both before and after 9 August, while accusing the other of falling into the fallacy of "post hoc, ergo propter hoc." When pressed honest proponents of both points of view may be forced to admit that their assessments of actual consequences and likelihoods are based at least as much on speculation as on hard evidence. Thus, utilitarian arguments may not settle all disagreements, but they may help to eliminate unnecessary disagreements and to identify precise points of difference. They may also help to establish the point that this is a topic on which reasonable men can honestly and honourably disagree.

principles for legislation

There are four principles which should govern the formulation of an emergency powers statute within the common law tradition. First that the provisions of any such legislation should involve the minimum necessary derogation from common law rights ; secondly that emergency powers should be brought into operation only to the extent which is strictly required by a given emergency ; thirdly that maximum safeguards should be provided in respect both of the introduction of each individual power and of its exercise ; and fourthly that all emergency powers should be clearly and precisely formulated so that the security authorities are not left to operate under the existing vague and general common law powers.

The first two of these principles are closely related. If emergency powers legislation involving a measure of derogation from ordinary common law rights can only be justified by the existence of an emergency, it follows that only that degree of derogation is justified which is necessitated by the particular emergency. (" A regulation which creates an offence so wide in its terms as to make unlawful conduct which cannot have the effect of endangering the preservation of the peace and the maintenance of order is not in my view rendered valid merely because the description of the conduct penalised is also wide enough to embrace conduct which is reasonably likely to have that effect." Lord Diplock dissenting in *McEldowney v Forde*, 1971 AC, 632, pp 661-2.) Thus it is not the case that any emergency will justify the suspension of all common law rights. The burden should rather be placed on those who would invoke emergency powers to show that there is an emergency situation endangering the peace of the community which cannot be resolved without the suspension of specified common law rights. This can only be operated if there is formal provision for the individual implementation of each of the powers included in an emergency powers act.

The third principle may be justified on a number of related grounds. First there is a general argument from the conception of justice rooted in the common law tradition. The decision as to whether the requirements of substantive justice have been met is frequently determined, in whole or in part, by inquiring into whether the requirements of procedural justice have been met. Typically, the invocation of emergency powers legislation is not motivated by a desire to deny substantive justice to anyone. Rather it is to remove certain safeguards which the common law has evolved to guarantee procedural justice. It is, therefore, clear that in common law jurisdictions it is assumed that the presence of procedural safeguards is conducive to the realization of substantive justice, and the greater the degree to which procedural safeguards are ignored the more likely it becomes that the ends of substantive justice will be frustrated. We have taken the view that this argument is applicable equally to emergency powers as to normal police powers, and have thus sought in our proposals to introduce procedural safeguards which will help to meet the requirements of justice without rendering the powers which they qualify useless.

Procedural safeguards in respect of emergency powers may also be justified on more pragmatic grounds. In any situation where a significant sector of the population is of the opinion that normal legal and political channels are no longer effectively open to them it is of the greatest importance to restore their confidence in lawful procedures. It is not necessary in this context to debate the factual issue as to whether legal and political channels in Northern Ireland have been and are effectively open to the minority community. The argument is rather that unless all sections of the community believe that the political and legal structures will protect their interests and impartially settle their disputes there is little prospect of normalising the situation. This applies equally to the introduction of emergency powers. It will probably not be possible to convince everyone in the community of the need for emergency powers on the basis of a particular interpretation of the facts. But it may be possible to convince them at least that the procedure by which that factual decision was made was fair and impartial and thus to accept the result more willingly. This suggests that wherever possible a procedure be provided by which the sceptical may challenge the interpretation of the facts adopted by the authorities.

The very fact that procedural and administrative safeguards are built into an emergency powers act may in itself induce the authorities to adopt a cautious approach to the wholesale use of powers which have been granted to them. To take a simple example, if the power to intern without trial is permitted only on the condition that those interned shall be entitled to a standard of comfort and to facilities which are not generally accorded to convicted prisoners, this in itself may cause the authorities to hesitate before deciding to intern a very large number of people. Similarly the existence of a readily accessible procedure by which complaints against the abuse of discretionary powers may be redressed will encourage some measure of caution in their use. There is no way to ensure that discretionary powers will not be abused. But such abuses are less likely to occur if those who make use of the powers are directly accountable for their actions.

The final principle that all emergency powers should be clearly and precisely formulated is directly related to the question of redress. The more general a power, the more difficult it is to establish that it has been abused. Again to take a simple example it might be argued that in emergency conditions there was a common law right to impose a curfew or to detain suspected insurgents for questioning for a reasonable period. A well drafted emergency powers act, however, will typically set precise limits on any such power to impose a curfew or to detain for questioning, and will thus both set a standard for the security authorities and also facilitate an aggrieved person in seeking redress where those standards are infringed.

The fundamental justification for the adoption of all these principles, however, is that if they are ignored the effect of emergency powers legislation is likely to be the arbitrary exercise of power and the intimidation of a disaffected minority in the Northern Ireland context. Only if the principles are accepted are those concerned likely to use legal rather than violent avenues of protest and complaint. The way to reintegrate a disaffected minority is not to remove all procedures through which they can challenge the legitimacy of the authority exercised over them, but to provide an avenue for obtaining satisfaction so that they are less likely to support those who would resort to gelignite. Civil order obtained through intimidation rather than integration will ensure the continuing need for emergency powers. The objective of introducing emergency powers is rather to create a situation in which they are no longer required.

4. emergency powers

The application of these general principles to each of the powers which the executive may claim to be necessary or desirable in dealing with an outbreak of subversion or other violent political activity and their reduction to statutory form is discussed below under various different headings.

Powers under all these heads should not necessarily be included in any emergency powers legislation, nor should they all be granted to the authorities in the special conditions prevailing in Northern Ireland. But it is desirable to set out as comprehensively as possible the arguments for and against the provision of the full range of powers and procedures for dealing with an emergency which have been applied in other common law jurisdictions, and also to give some account of the way in which these powers might be reduced to statutory form.

This list of heads for discussion is restricted to powers designed to deal with deliberate subversion of a violent nature. We are aware of the fineness of the line between deliberate violence of this kind and that which may arise out of civil commotion and some forms of allegedly non-violent political protest, and of the special need for controls over "provocative" demonstrations and processions in Northern Ireland. But though there may be some overlap in the powers which the authorities may reasonably demand to deal with these two forms of political violence, we feel that a very clear distinction should be made between powers to deal with deliberate and violent subversion on the one hand and outwardly peaceful protest and civil disobedience on the other. The general issues which arise in connection with the control of public meetings, processions and other forms of peaceful protest and demonstration are therefore discussed separately below.

martial law

It is established law in common law jurisdictions that where a situation of armed insurrection exists the forces of the Crown may take the law into their own hands by establishing military courts or even *in extremis* resorting to summary execution of insurgents or their supporters. It is usual in such cases for the authorities to make a declaration of martial law but legally this is unnecessary in that it is the existence of a situation in which the ordinary courts of the land cannot operate effectively or at all rather than any formal declaration which justifies the resort to extra-legal procedures and sanctions. Furthermore the implementation of martial law, whether declared or not, does not as is often assumed constitute a total suspension of the common law. The position is rather that the exigencies of the situation may be deemed at common law to justify what may be thought of as actions by way of self-help or self-defence on the part of the authorities.

These actions may therefore be called in question after the event in the courts which will determine in any case raised before them whether or not the precise procedures and sanctions used by the authorities or the precise degree of force used by individual members of the armed forces were or were not justified in all the circumstances; if they are not found to have been justified the courts will apply the ordinary sanctions by way of damages or criminal penalties. In practical terms, however, subsequent review of the behaviour of the authorities under martial law conditions is usually excluded by the enactment of a statute of indemnity granting retrospective or prospective legal immunity to all persons acting on behalf of the authorities against any legal proceedings arising out of their treatment of those suspected of terrorist activities or sympathies.

There has to date been no declaration of martial law in the current Northern Ireland crisis, and no attempt to introduce a statute of indemnity, either at Westminster or at Stormont. (The Northern Ireland Act 1972 does explicitly authorise the Northern Ireland legislature to introduce a measure of indemnity in respect both of its own security forces and of the armed forces of the Crown.) It is nonetheless arguable that some of the activities of the security authorities have only been legally justifiable either on the grounds that some form of martial law might be deemed to be in force, or on the basis of the residual common law powers of military intervention to preserve public order or to prevent serious injury to persons or to property. The declaration of a curfew by the military forces in the Lower Falls area in July 1970, for instance, was subsequently upheld in a magistrate's court as a reasonable exercise of common law powers in an emergency situation. Furthermore in the case of some of the shooting incidents involving the security forces, even if the precise instruction of the "yellow card" issued to each individual soldier, which is a broadly accurate statement of the common law powers of any citizen, had not been observed it would be open to a court to hold that it had no jurisdiction to hear any action against the soldier concerned on the ground that a state of martial law existed.

The law in this sphere is not clearly settled. Many of the cases are outdated and vague, and an overall review of the position is long overdue. (See for example *Marais v General Officer Commanding,* 1902, AC, 109; *R v Strickland* 1921, 2, IR, 317, *Wright v Fitzgerald,* 1799, 27, St Tr, 765, *Higgins v Willis,* 1921, 2, IR, 386, *R v Allen* 1921, 2, IR, 241, *Egan v Macready,* 1921, 1, IR, 265, *Re Clifford and O'Sullivan,* 1921, 2 AC, 570, see generally, 18, LQR, 117, 133, 152 (1902), and R. F. V. Heuston, *Essays in constitutional law,* pp 150-158 for a discussion of the Irish decisions on martial law.) The line of argument that martial law is in force, however, has not been relied on by the security authorities either on a political or a legal level. In most cases explicit reliance has been placed on the powers conferred on the security forces, both civil and military, by the Special Powers Act and Regulations thereunder. Thus when certain of these regulations were held by the Northern Ireland Divisional Court to be *ultra vires* the Northern Ireland legislature immediate action was taken by the British Government in the Northern Ireland Act 1972 to restore the position to what it was generally believed in Whitehall to have been prior to that decision. (*The Queen* v *The Justices of the Peace for the County of the City of Londonderry, ex parte Hume et al.,* Queen's Bench Division (Crown Side) Divisional Court, 23 February 1972.) We accept that this general approach is the correct one in all the circumstances. To rely on martial law powers of arrest and search in a situation when the ordinary courts and legal processes were still very clearly operating would be to expose the armed forces to a wholly unacceptable degree of uncertainty as to the legality of their activities. In addition the peculiar circumstances of the Northern Ireland situation demand a level of clarity and certainty in the extent of the emergency powers in the hands of the authorities which cannot be achieved by reliance on common law or martial law powers. We have thus rejected the argument that common law and martial law powers are sufficient to deal with any emergency, and have accepted that emergency powers legislation is necessary.

declaring a state of emergency

In many countries where there is a written constitution conferring fundamental rights on its citizens there is also provision for the declaration of a state of emergency under which some or all of those fundamental rights may be suspended or revoked. Similarly under most international conventions guaranteeing fundamental individual rights, such as the European Convention on Human Rights, there is provision for the suspension of some of those rights by derogation on the part of the signatory country in a state of emergency. In most countries where this type of constitutional guarantee is adopted there is some formal control over the declaration of a state of emergency by the executive either by legislative or judicial organs. The Federal Constitution of Malaysia is an instance of legislative control. the Constitution provides for a Proclamation of Emergency by the King (the Yang di-Pertuan Agong) where the security or economic life of the Federation is threatened; the King may then issue ordinances of any kind which shall be valid regardless of any inconsistency with other provisions of the Constitution (article 150); but any such proclamation may be annulled by resolution of both houses of the legislature; the legislature may also circumvent this procedure by the enactment of measures reciting the objective of containing organised violence, disaffection, hostility between races, the alteration by unlawful means of legal institutions, or the security of the Federation, which overrides any other constitutional guarantees and which may not be contested in any court (article 149).

Again, under the Anglo-Rhodesian settlement proposals (Cmnd 4835, 1971) a proclamation of a state of public emergency will lapse if it has not been approved by resolution of the House of Assembly within 7 days if the House is sitting, or within 30 days in any other case. Furthermore, the House may at any time resolve that a declaration of emergency should be revoked and if such a resolution is approved, the President shall forthwith revoke the declaration (Rhodesian Constitution, 1969, section 61.)

Similarly under the Irish Offences Against the State Act 1940, which authorises the internment of individuals without trial, provision is made for a prior proclamation that the implementation of that power is necessary to secure public peace and order; any such proclamation however may be annulled by resolution of Dail Eireann upon which the power to intern lapses immediately (section 3); in this case there is no exclusion of judicial review, so that an application could presumably be made to the courts to declare the Proclamation invalid as having been made in bad faith or on wholly unreasonable grounds. The best example of purely judicial review, however, is that under the European Convention on Human Rights: in the *Lawless Case* (1957) the European Court held that though the introduction of powers of internment in the Republic of Ireland had been justifiable in all the circumstances, the grounds for any derogation from the Convention could be inquired into by the Court and that if they were found to be inadequate the derogation and any infringement of individual rights under it would be deemed to be a breach of the Convention.

In Britain this form of legislation is not usually adopted in view of the absence of a written constitution and the doctrine of parliamentary sovereignty under which the government of the day may at any time press through an emergency statute providing powers to deal with any security situation which may arise, as in the Defence of the Realm Act 1914. But the proclamation system has been adopted under the Emergency Powers Acts 1920 and 1964 for emergencies resulting from industrial action, and any such declaration is subject to annulment by a negative resolution in either House.

In Northern Ireland the above approach has been pushed to its furthest extent in security matters by the enactment of permanent security powers under the Special Powers Act. This statute could at any time have been repealed by act of the Stormont Parliament, or indeed by the Westminster Parliament, and regulations issued under the Acts could have been annulled by the Governor if within 14 days of the laying of the regulation before Parliament, one of the Houses prays that it be annulled. But in the special circumstances of more or less permanent one party rule this was not an effective safeguard. The fact that the legislature effectively transferred the power to legislate in security matters to the executive in so far as is possible under British constitutional doctrine is one of the major complaints against the Act. In addition the possibility of effective judicial review on the ground of excess of jurisdiction by the executive has been largely negated by the decision of the House of Lords in *McEldowney v Forde* (1971, AC, 632) that a regulation (24a) banning all "republican clubs or any like organisation howsoever described" was not an unreasonable use of the power to make regulations for peace and order within Northern Ireland.

In a situation where there is a divided community, as in Northern Ireland, it would seem that there is a strong case for imposing more effective controls over the initiation of emergency powers. The form of control depends largely on the wider political decision as to the allocation of security powers over Northern Ireland. If a new Emergency Powers (Security) Act is enacted for the whole of the United Kingdom, as suggested below, then a simple legislative control requiring the ratification at Westminster of the declaration of an emergency within Northern Ireland might be acceptable. But if power of control over internal security is left in the hands of the executive within the context of a Northern Ireland legislature, then a simple legislative safeguard of this kind would not be sufficient given the history of sectarian politics within the Province. There are two alternatives which would provide an additional safeguard in this context. First the ratification of a declaration of emergency could be made dependent on the vote of at least two thirds of all elected members, whether present or not, so that a simple majority governing party could not on its own ratify a decision of its own executive. Secondly control might be given to a judicial review body with full power to hear the evidence from the security authorities and to determine whether the declaration of the emergency was in all the circumstances justified. This form of control would not be likely to be acceptable within a sovereign state such as the United Kingdom, but might be workable in the Northern Ireland context given the possibility of a constitutional settlement guaranteed by both the United Kingdom and the Republic of Ireland.

If a settlement of this kind were made, or if a more far reaching form of condominium by the United Kingdom and the Republic of Ireland over Northern Ireland were instituted, then the appointment of a judicial review body with representatives of both guaranteeing powers and perhaps a Commonwealth or European president would be a convenient means of securing control over the declaration of an emergency. Any such declaration by the executive, however constituted, would then be referred automatically to the review body and the emergency powers conferred under it would lapse if the declaration were not confirmed by the review body within the specified period of time.

Further provision is also required to control the termination of the emergency. The simplest formulation in this context is probably to restrict any declaration to a period of six months or a year, and to impose the same controls over the extension of a declared emergency as over its initiation.

emergency offences

It is implicit in the declaration of an emergency and the creation of emergency powers that the ordinary processes of the criminal law are inadequate to deal with the situation. The bulk of emergency legislation has typically dealt with powers of arrest and search and of preventive detention. But this emphasis should not exclude consideration of the creation of emergency offences which either extend the ambit of criminal conduct or permit some derogation from the ordinary procedural and evidential rules governing criminal trials. This approach has particular advantages in the Northern Ireland situation in that preventive detention or internment is now a highly emotive issue on which it is virtually impossible to reach a compromise agreement between representatives of the different groups. More generally the creation of new offences designed specifically to deal with those involved in subversive movements has the advantage that if there is a resolution of the political issues which occasioned a particular emergency, the declaration of an amnesty for all those convicted of offences under the emergency legislation is made administratively and psychologically easier.

Existing criminal law makes provision for the conviction of those involved in certain types of subversive activity over and above the ordinary range of criminal offences dealing with injury to persons and damage to property through the common law offences of treason and sedition. In broad terms treason covers any attempt by force or other illegal means to overthrow the government of the state, and sedition the encouragement or incitement of any such attempt by public speeches or other forms of propaganda. There is ample precedent for the use of these offences against the leaders of movements in Ireland in the course of the nineteenth century. But there are serious drawbacks in relying on these common law offences. As in the case of martial law there is no clear understanding as to the precise extent of the law, and there is a natural tendency to regard the offences of treason and sedition as restricted to the leaders of a particular movement, and a consequent likelihood of acquittal if they are employed against those lower down in the hierarchy of the movement. The common law offence of conspiracy does permit proceedings to be brought against such persons against whom there is no proof of active participation in individual attacks on persons or property, but a conviction for such a charge requires direct proof of the involvement of those charged in the planning or presentation of those individual attacks. And since direct evidence of this kind is not easy to obtain, there may be no ready means of bringing proceedings against those in middle and lower command positions in subversive organisations.

One solution to this dilemma is to make mere membership of certain organisations illegal as discussed in the next section. But there may also be advantages in the enactment of offences covering the broad range of subversive activity in more specific terms than under the existing offences of treason and sedition. The type of activity which might be specified in this way would be the promotion or incitement of the use of violence against persons or property, and the raising or training or organisation of groups or individuals for such purposes (see below). Such activities are in theory covered by the existing common law offence of incitement and by the sections of the Public Order Acts dealing with para-military organisations, but an explicit prohibition under emergency legislation would allow them to be dealt with more directly and also, as discussed below, for certain changes in procedural and evidential rules to be made to permit a more effective balance between protecting the innocent and convicting the guilty in the special conditions of intimidation or communal division which may prevail.

the proscription of illegal organisations

The proscription of subversive or anti-government organisations has long been the first line of attack adopted by the authorities in emergency situations. The formulation in the Special Powers Act is typical of many other jurisdictions, in giving absolute discretion to the executive to ban any organisation, membership of which thus becomes in itself an offence. The advantage of this strategy from the point of view of the authorities is clear, in that no evidence of illegal activity other than membership of the proscribed organisation need be sought. But the dangers of abuse are equally clear in that the power may be used to suppress legitimate political opposition to the existing government by those committed to non-violent or constitutional methods of protest and opposition. This point is especially relevant in Northern Ireland where all republican organisations have been regarded by the authorities as subversive regardless of their stance on the methods to be employed in the pursuit of their objective of the unification of Ireland.

Nevertheless, we recognize that there is a purpose in banning subversive organisations in that this makes it possible for the authorities to hamper their activities and to bring charges against their officers and members. But if the executive is given a discretionary power to ban named organisations this should not be unrestricted. Only those organisations which engage in or incite violent subversive activity to accomplish political ends should be subject to the executive ban. Organisations which disagree with governmental policies but which advocate change through constitutional processes should not be subject to a ban. To ensure that this principle is adhered to the grounds for a declaration of illegality should be clearly formulated and provision made for review in the courts. The provisions of the

Offences Against the State Act 1939 of the Irish Republic are a good example. This provides that "any organisation which: (a) engages in, promotes, encourages or advocates the commission of treason or any activity of a treasonable nature, or (b) advocates, encourages or attempts the procuring by force, violence or other unconstitutional means of an alteration of the constitution, or (c) raises or maintains, or attempts to raise or maintain a military or armed force in contravention of the constitution or without constitutional authority, or (d) engages in, promotes, encourages, or advocates the commission of any criminal offences or the obstruction of or interference with the administration of justice or the enforcement of the law, or (e) engages in, promotes, encourages or advocates the attainment of any particular objective, lawful or unlawful, by violent, criminal or other unlawful means, or (f) promotes, encourages or advocates the non-payment of moneys payable to the Central Fund or any other public fund or the non-payment of local taxation shall be an unlawful organisation" (section 18); any such organisation may be declared to be such by the Government under section 19, but there is provision in section 20 for any interested person to make an application to the High Court for a declaration that a particular organisation is not illegal under the terms of section 18 despite a governmental declaration to the contrary. Membership of an illegal organisation is then made a criminal offence in itself, though there is a defence of lack of knowledge of its unlawful nature. (It is questionable whether the definition of unlawful objects or activities for this purpose should extend to the prohibition of civil disobedience, as provided in the Irish Act—see below.)

Imposing sanctions on the basis of membership in unlawful organisations poses serious problems in the absence of clear standards of "membership." For example, the mere appearance of a name on membership rolls or lists of contributors should not be sufficient evidence to convict, or to transfer the burden of proof to the defendant. Frequently, organisations of the type we are concerned with, will gain financial and other forms of support through threats and intimidation. It is highly unlikely that a person who has contributed to such an organisation as a result of threats, will be able to prove this upon being charged with being a member of the unlawful organisation. We suggest, therefore, that for the purposes of emergency powers legislation, "membership" be defined in terms of knowing and voluntary participation in the activities of a banned organisation. "Participation" should be construed as requiring overt actions and although the appearance of a name on membership rolls or lists of contributors may be evidence of participation in the activities of the unlawful organisation, such evidence should not be sufficient to convict or transfer the burden of proof. The officers or office bearers of unlawful organisations would presumably be the main concern of an attempt to suppress the activities of an unlawful organisation. If being an officer or office bearer in an unlawful organisation is to constitute a criminal offence, then it should be the case that the evidence of such status be limited to activity performed in that capacity for or on behalf of the organisation. In other words, a person cannot be guilty of being an officer in an unlawful organisation unless there is evidence to show that he has acted in that capacity.

subversive literature and documents

Similar considerations arise in respect of subversive literature and documents. It is important to preserve the right to campaign by peaceful and constitutional means for changes in the political and economic order without facilitating the promotion and organisation of subversion and violence. Though some codes of emergency powers do contain general provisions permitting the banning of particular publications, as in regulation 8 of the Special Powers Act, most are restricted to the contents of particular issues or items, or to the prohibition of literature and documents produced by prohibited organisations, as in regulation 24A of the Special Powers Act. The most appropriate strategy would seem to be to define seditious literature and documents as those which contain material advocating violence or other subversive activities, but not peaceful protest or civil disobedience, or which seek to encourage recruitment for illegal organisations, and then to make it an explicit criminal offence for any person to be concerned in the preparation, printing, publication or distribution of any such literature or documents. Mere possession of seditious literature or documents on the other hand should not be an offence. The distinction to be drawn, as in the case of membership of illegal organisations, is between active involvement and passive interest or sympathy. Any attempt at prosecution in the latter case may well do more harm than good, in that the individual may not realise the illegality or may have had the documents pressed on him by activists, or may have them for innocuous reasons.

questioning prior to arrest

Where a campaign of violent terrorist attacks has been instituted some derogation from the ordinary common law rule that no person shall be required to answer any questions as to his identity or movements at any time may be necessary if the security authorities are to be able to take preventive action. The existing regulation under the Special Powers Act confers power on any member of the security forces to stop and ask any person any questions which may reasonably be addressed to him, and the failure to answer to the best of his ability and knowledge constitutes an offence (regulation 7). In addition any person may be arrested without warrant and detained for a period of up to 48 hours for the purpose of interrogation (regulation 10). The objection to these provisions is not their existence, but the lack of any ready means by which their use may be controlled and abuses corrected.

There are numerous precedents for imposing an obligation in normal times on any person to establish his identity when required to do so by an authorised person, and for according a power of arrest in cases where there is reasonable suspicion that a false name and address has been given. There is unlikely to be any serious difficulty in formulating such a power to the satisfaction of all. It is more difficult to decide how far beyond this power it is reasonable to go for the purposes of combating a terrorist campaign. There would appear to be two broad grounds on which an extension might be based: first to enable security forces to require any person to give an account of his reason for being where he is stopped, and second to enable them to require a person to give an account of his movements at any particular time. The first of these is essentially a preventive measure to permit the authorities to forestall terrorist activity, the second an aid to the clearing up of attacks which have already taken place. For this reason it is suggested that any statutory formulation should make a distinction between the obligation to give a simple account of physical movement in specified periods in the past, and the obligation to give an account of the reasons for being in a particular place at the time of questioning.

detention for questioning

Where an authorised person has reason to suspect that a person has not given a full and truthful account in answer to questions posed under these two heads, or where a person seeks to evade or obstruct the posing of such questions, further power to arrest and detain for questioning may reasonably be sought by the authorities. The usual limit on such detention is 48 hours. Where this further questioning suggests that an offence has been committed, or that the answers given previously by the person detained were not true, then the suspect may be charged of a substantive offence and brought before the courts, where the question of further detention or release on bail may be dealt with in the usual way. Power to take photographs and fingerprints of any person, as in section 30 of the Offences Against the State Act 1939 of the Irish Republic, might also, very well, be added in this context.

The most difficult issues in this context are those of the treatment of persons detained for questioning, and the review of cases of alleged ill-treatment or the abuse of the power to detain. The government has accepted that certain forms of ill-treatment in the course of questioning are neither legal nor permissible, as recommended in the minority report of the Parker Committee (*Report of the Committee of Privy Councillors appointed to consider authorised procedures for the interrogation of persons suspected of terrorism,* Cmnd 4901, March 1972) but safeguards are still necessary. The most effective are likely to be the enactment of specific regulations governing the treatment of those detained for questioning, and the creation of a review tribunal with power to award compensation to those whose complaints are found to be justified. The details of regulations to govern the questioning of persons detained need not be discussed here. But the principles upon which they should be formulated are clear: first that the conditions under which questioning may take place should be specified, including the permitted length of periods of questioning, and provision for sleep and refreshment; second that persons detained should be granted access to legal advice of their choice; and thirdly that provision should be made for medical inspection of all persons both before and after and supervision during the period of questioning.

In respect of the review of complaints of the abuse of the power to detain for questioning two broad principles might be adopted: first that the infringement of ordinary rights which the grant of such a power constitutes be recognised by provision for the compensation for loss of employment or earnings of all persons detained against whom charges are not subsequently preferred; and second that the ordinary procedures for civil action for the abuse of powers be simplified by permitting a simple claim against the authorities to be registered before a specially appointed tribunal which should have power to order compensation not only for loss of earnings incurred as a result of the detention, but also for the loss of liberty or any ill-treatment suffered in breach of the regulations governing questioning, as for instance where it could be shown that no reasonable grounds for the detention of the person in question could be produced by the authorities. The constitution and procedures for such a tribunal are further discussed below, but the principle on which they are based is that the increase in the powers of the authorities should be offset by making it easier for claims of abuse to be established.

arrest

Given the existence of a power to arrest and detain for questioning and the creation of a range of emergency criminal offences, there should be no need for a more general emergency power of arrest. An emergency powers statute would simply make all emergency offences arrestable under the Criminal Law Act, 1966, or the Criminal Law Act (NI), 1967 so that any person reasonably suspected of having committed an offence could be arrested without warrant. Provision for an expedited complaints and compensation procedure in cases where the authorities could be shown to have acted unreasonably would also apply, as discussed below. It should also be noted that ordinary legal procedures in respect of the granting or refusal of bail would apply to persons charged with offences under the emergency powers statute, so that the authorities should not be able to make use of unreasonable holding charges as an alternative to detention without trial. The position in this respect would be no different from that currently applicable in Northern Ireland where there have been a number of cases in which magistrates or the High Court have granted applications for bail against the wishes of the authorities (see for example the case of *Close* in December 1971 in which the magistrate's decision to grant bail was subsequently upheld by the High Court, and borne out by the fact that at the trial all charges not previously withdrawn were withdrawn from consideration by the jury on the ground of lack of any credible evidence). The existence of the Special Powers Act, however, has permitted the authorities to detain and intern some of those whose release has been ordered by the courts. The retention of formal judicial control in this sphere is therefore an important part of the general strategy of granting adequate powers to the security authorities but subjecting their exercise to searching independent control. There is no reason to believe that the courts will not be anxious to co-operate with the authorities in any case where there is any reason to suspect that the release of a suspect might not be in the public interest.

search and seizure

The power to search for and to seize firearms and explosives is already granted to the authorities under permanent legislation. In addition there is a general common law power to search for and seize evidence of the commission of serious offences whether or not a warrant has been obtained (*Chic Fashions (West Wales) Ltd v Jones,* 1968, 2 QB, 299). But in view of the unsettled state of the law in this and other related respects, and of the advantages of legal clarity in emergency conditions, a new emergency powers statute should include an explicit power to search for and to seize without warrant any objects or documents designed or intended for use in contravention of the emergency legislation, or which would constitute admissible evidence of the commission of an offence before the emergency criminal court. As in the case of other extended powers granted in connection with the emergency, the expedited and simplified procedures for dealing with complaints of abuse and for awarding compensation for any loss or injury unreasonably inflicted by the authorities would apply.

detention without trial

The most far-reaching power likely to be demanded by the authorities in an emergency situation short of open hostilities with a foreign power is the right to intern without trial any person suspected of being a security risk. Powers under this general head may extend from relatively minor restriction orders or house arrest to full scale internment in camps prepared for the purpose. Under the Special Powers Act use has sometimes been made of full scale internment, but simpler restriction orders were also used in the prewar period, often with the implicit objective of forcing the person concerned to go into voluntary exile. (Regulation 12 authorises the Minister of Home Affairs to require any person "to remain in, or to proceed to and reside in, such place as may be specified in the order and to comply with such directions as to reporting to the police, restriction of movement and otherwise as may be specified . . . or to be interned." For examples of the use of restriction orders see *Report of a commission of inquiry,* National Council of Civil Liberties, 1936, pp 19 and 37.) All forms of the power, however, may be regarded as the most serious infringement of ordinary rights yet considered in that the ultimate decision on the liberty of those involved is typically made by the executive either on evidence which would not stand up in a court or else on the basis of what the suspect might do in the future rather than what he has already done. In addition the power of internment has acquired a highly emotive connotation in Northern Ireland from the history of its almost exclusive use against one section of the community and the lack of a clear distinction in its implementation between violent and political opposition to the existing regime. Moreover, once the initial decision was taken to introduce a policy of internment in August 1971, it was implemented on a very substantial scale and in a manner which has been subject to much criticism, even by those who were not opposed to internment in principle. The large numbers selected for internment, the conditions at the holding centres and Long Kesh, the speed and adequacy of the procedures for review and the lack of other safeguards have all given cause for concern, even among those who believe that the decision of August 9th was justified. It is our view that internment is an extreme measure which should be used, if at all, on an extremely limited scale, subject to rigorous safeguards and in a manner that ensures that as far as is feasible internees are treated conspicuously better than ordinary prisoners. If this kind of means must be used, it is important that adequate resources should be provided to mitigate it and to ensure that it is implemented in as civilised a manner as possible. We do not wish to argue that a power of internment can never be justified in any circumstances, but we have nonetheless adopted the position that it should be avoided wherever possible and that it should not be further used in Northern Ireland.

The power of internment may be sought by the authorities for two broad reasons: first because of the difficulty of securing convictions against those known or suspected of being involved in subversive activities; and secondly in order to prevent future subversion by those thought likely to resort to it. These two heads of justification cannot always be clearly distinguished in individual cases, but it is useful to consider what may be termed preventive and punitive internment separately both in relation to the current situation in Northern Ireland and in the preparation of a new general framework for emergency powers.

The need to resort to punitive internment is frequently justified by the impossibility of securing convictions in the courts either because of the difficulty in obtaining evidence against suspects or else because of the fear which the potential witnesses may have of reprisals against themselves or their families if they give evidence in court. This is a very real danger in Northern Ireland in that the murder of potential witnesses and informers is established practice among subversive groups. (The most blatant recent case was the assassination on 18 January 1972 of Mr. Sidney Agnew the day before he was due to give evidence of the hijacking of a bus.) We have sought to meet these difficulties by combination of provision for the hearing of cases in camera and other procedural and evidential rules within the framework of specially constituted emergency courts, as discussed below, and the creation of a range of emergency offences specifically designed to deal with those who have overtly shown their support for or involvement in subversive activities. On balance therefore we have recommended that those suspected of actual involvement in violent subversion should be dealt with by formal charges rather than by internment without trial. We feel that this approach is likely to prove *more* effective in meeting the requirements of security, especially in Northern Ireland, since it denies to subversive groups the ready recruiting platform that internment without trial affords.

We have adopted a similar position in respect of purely preventive internment. This has regularly been employed under the Special Powers Act against those thought to be likely to resort to subversive activities on the evidence of their past associations or actions without seeking to prove that they have actually done anything to deserve detention in the immediate emergency. The use of the Special Powers Act for this purpose has been one of the principal and most cogent objections to the current security operation, in that a number of persons have been interned who are generally believed by their families and associates and therefore by their local communities not to have been involved in any form of violent subversion, and who thus appear to have been imprisoned for their political views rather than for their actions. Given the essentially political nature of the conflict in Northern Ireland this has probably had a wholly counterproductive effect. Having made this assessment of the current situation, we have been faced with the difficult question whether or not to make provision for powers of detention without trial in a new general emergency powers statute of the kind which we have suggested. Two views might reasonably be adopted in this context: first that provision should be made for detention without trial so that if it is ever necessary to resort to it an adequate range of controls and safeguards will have been built in to the enabling statute in advance; and secondly that a power of internment should not be included on the ground that it is undesirable to make advance provision for and thus to facilitate the implementation of a power which should only be adopted in the last resort. We have resolved this dilemma in favour of the second alternative on the pragmatic ground that the twin effect of the emotive significance of internment in Northern Ireland and the traditional dislike of any such power in Britain as a whole would be likely to cause serious difficulties in securing parliamentary approval for the kind of emergency powers legislation which we envisage.

It is nonetheless important to include some discussion of the range and type of safeguards which should in our view be adopted if a power of detention without trial were to be included or subsequently adopted. The principles upon which these safeguards should be based are firstly that specific prior authorisation be granted for the implementation of powers to intern without trial separately and distinct from the implementation of other emergency powers; secondly that the evidence upon which a person is detained, whether it relates to past activities or to the likelihood of future involvement in subversion, should be reviewed by a judicial body independent of those whose responsibility it is to implement the power; thirdly that wherever possible an opportunity be given to the suspect to refute that evidence and to be allowed representation for that purpose; fourthly that a procedure for compensating those interned and their dependents be established; fifthly that detailed regulations for the treatment of internees and for their rights in respect of visits be published; and finally that provision be made for full disclosure both to their families and to the public at large of the names of all those interned as soon as is reasonably practicable. Each of these points may be dealt with briefly in turn:

1. *Prior sanction*: the nature of this prior control would depend on the form of control adopted for the declaration of an emergency but whatever form is adopted the special position of detention without trial should be recognised by provision for a separate and distinct procedure for authorising its implementation, whether by a special affirmative resolution, a special majority or otherwise.

2. *Judicial review*: the justification for the detention of each internee should be automatically and periodically reviewed within a specified period by a judicial tribunal with full jurisdiction to hear the evidence upon which the authorities seek to justify the detention, to subpoena witnesses, and come to their own decision on the merits. There is provision (regulation 12 (3)) under the Special Powers Act for the review of each case by an advisory committee, but the Civil Authority is under no obligation to accept a recommendation for release. The provisions of the Irish Offences Against the State Act 1940, are a better precedent in this respect in that the Commission which must be set up as soon as internment is implemented has power to order the release of any internee if it appears that there is no reasonable ground for his continued detention; this provision was introduced in 1940 after judicial proceedings had established that the provisions of the 1939 Act were unconstitutional (s8).

3. *Right of representation*: each internee should have a right to appear and to be represented before the tribunal. To enable him to refute any false or inaccurate allegations made to the tribunal by the authorities he should be given a full statement of the grounds upon which he is interned and the evidence against him, subject only to the right of the authorities to petition the tribunal that the source of the evidence need not be revealed. An undertaking that the grounds for internment shall be revealed and that each internee shall have the right to be represented has been given by the Ministry of Home Affairs in Northern Ireland, though there have been complaints about the stereotyped nature of the reasons given. It is suggested that this undertaking should be made a statutory obligation, and that the objection as to the stereotyped nature of the reasons given be met by the obligation to reveal the evidence against each internee.

4. *Compensation*: given that detention without trial is adopted as a preventive rather than a punitive measure, those detained should be compensated by the community for whose alleged benefit they

have been deprived of their liberty. The simplest and most acceptable measure of compensation for this purpose is perhaps a payment to the dependents of the person detained sufficient to maintain them as they would have been maintained if the breadwinner had not been removed. Consideration should also be given to the payment of compensation to any trade or business which suffers unavoidable loss through the detention of any of its principals.

5. *Disclosure*: full and regular disclosure should also be made of the identity of those detained and the relatives or dependents of any person detained should be informed within a specified time.

6. *Conditions of detention*: specific regulations should be adopted and published governing the conditions of detention along the lines of prison rules but providing for better conditions, as for instance under the Offences Against the State Act 1940.

special courts

If a power of detention without trial is generally to be denied to the authorities in emergency conditions, it is important to ensure that those suspected of subversive activities can be brought quickly to trial, and that those who are guilty will not escape conviction on procedural or technical grounds. In addition action may be necessary to counteract the possibility of the intimidation of witnesses or juries. The approach to this problem which appears most likely to prove satisfactory is to remove the trial of emergency offences from the ordinary courts when they cannot adequately deal with the situation, and to establish a temporary emergency court or courts whose procedure and rules of evidence are more appropriate to the conditions prevailing in the community. This may involve some derogation from the accepted common law rights of accused persons, but if the much more drastic derogation involved in the adoption of detention without trial is to be avoided some action to shift emphasis in rules of evidence and procedure away from the protection of the innocent towards the conviction of the guilty may be acceptable. The precise form of these alterations in procedure should probably be left to the discretion of judicial authorities subject to parliamentary approval by affirmative resolution of the rules which they propose to adopt. Some of the possibilities however may usefully be discussed briefly in this context:

Constitution of emergency courts: this is clearly dependent on the wider issue of the control of security and law and order, but in so far as Northern Ireland is concerned there would be clear advantages in ensuring the impartiality of any emergency court by the appointment of an external presiding judge, whether from Britain, Europe or the Commonwealth, and in providing that all cases shall be heard by a bench of at least two judges or magistrates.

Suspension of jury trial: where there is clear risk of intimidation or partial decisions by an ordinary jury, a risk which is of special relevance in a situation of communal conflict, the suspension of jury trial may well be necessary even for the most serious cases; as suggested above the objection to trial by any single judge or magistrate in serious cases may be met by provision for trial by a bench of judges or magistrates, or by a judge assisted by assessors.

Hearing in camera: to avoid unnecessary pressure on or danger to witnesses or to prevent the revelation of important sources of information the emergency court should be explicitly permitted to hear any case or part of any case in camera.

Rules of evidence: some alteration in the ordinary rules of evidence in criminal cases might be necessary to ensure that relevant evidence against a suspect was not excluded on grounds of technical inadmissability, as for instance by the suspension of the hearsay rule; if this were done, the final decision on the strength and credibility of the evidence would of course rest with the court; any derogation from the rules of evidence for this purpose should be regarded as an extreme measure.

Burden of proof: it might prove necessary in extreme circumstances to alter the traditional standard of proof in criminal cases, that the case be proved against the accused beyond reasonable doubt, to the somewhat less demanding standard of the balance of probability normally restricted to civil litigation.

Powers of disposal: where the nature of the charge against a suspect is of a preventive nature, as in the case of a charge of active involvement in an illegal organisation, a court which found the charge proved might be permitted to order indefinite detention of the accused until the termination of the emergency rather than to impose a definite sentence. It is also arguable that the maximum sentence for any emergency offence should be the duration of the emergency and that the authorities should be required to elect to proceed either in the emergency courts subject to this limitation or in the ordinary courts.

review tribunal

The basis of our proposal for the establishment of a special tribunal to deal with complaints over the misuse or abuse of emergency powers, as already explained, is that the additional powers granted to the security authorities should be offset by making it simpler for an aggrieved person to seek and gain redress for any injury or injustice suffered by him through the exercise of emergency powers. Though the common law action for unlawful assault or battery is available in all cases of unreasonable ill-treatment (see *Moore v Minister of Home Affairs,* Armagh County Court, February 1972), some acceleration in the somewhat dilatory processes of the ordinary civil courts is probably necessary to prevent allegations of maltreatment from themselves contributing to an escalation of the emergency.

In addition the tort of malicious prosecution imposes a very heavy burden of proof, that of establishing some lack of bona fides on the part of the defendants ; in the context of increased emergency powers of arrest and detention for questioning, this burden might reasonably be eased to require only evidence that the authorities acted unreasonably in all the circumstances. Similarly the ordinary rules as to compensation might be supplemented by a simplified scheme for the compensation for loss of employment or earnings of all persons detained against whom charges are not subsequently preferred, whether or not the action of the authorities could be shown to have been unreasonable in all the circumstances. As in the case of the special criminal courts discussed in the previous section, the formulation of rules of procedure and evidence should be left to the judicial authorities concerned, subject to parliamentary ratification. The constitution of such a review tribunal is similarly not a matter that can readily be prescribed in advance.

public order and civil disobedience

The main emphasis in this analysis of emergency powers has been on powers directed against violent subversion. But as was pointed out at the start of this chapter violent subversion cannot always be separated from the more general issues of public order and organised protest. Originally peaceful processions or meetings and other forms of non-violent protest or civil disobedience have on occasions been developed into violent confrontations. Such activities may in addition be closely connected with a campaign of violent subversion whether or not there is any direct relationship between the leaders of either movement. This is clearly a problem of special importance in Northern Ireland where there is a well established practice on all sides not just of organising mass processions and demonstrations, but also of seeking to assert some form of territorial supremacy by parading in areas where opposition may be expected. It is not surprising therefore that regulations have been adopted under the Special Powers Act authorising the control and prohibition of processions and meetings and other related matters. Specific legislation was also introduced by the Northern Ireland Parliament to deal with squatting in public buildings and other forms of civil disobedience (Public Order (Amendment) Act (NI), 1970). This legislation like the Special Powers Act is highly contentious, and the question arises as to whether any powers not already available under the ordinary law of public order should be included in an emergency powers statute to deal with this aspect of an emergency situation.

In so far as public order is concerned wherever possible the matter should be dealt with by permanent legislation. The existing strategy of the Public Order Acts of permitting the authorities to impose conditions as to routes and times for processions and as to time and place for meetings with a view to preventing disorder is broadly right. But in Northern Ireland it is clearly of the utmost importance that these decisions be made by a body which is accepted generally as impartial and independent. The statutory clarification of the somewhat vague common law rules on obstruction should be welcomed in that any confusion on the part of either the protesters or the authorities as to their respective rights increases rather than decreases the risk of unnecessary confrontations.

Nonetheless some increase in powers in this sphere may be necessary under emergency conditions. In particular a power to ban all processions in a particular area may be required, and when riot or civil disorder has already commenced it may be necessary to impose limited or extended forms of curfew or other restrictions on movement. As already stated it is our view that the existing common law powers in this respect are insufficiently clear, and that the need to rely on common law authority may impose an unnecessary burden of uncertainty on the authorities. We would thus recommend the inclusion in any emergency powers legislation of a general power to order restrictions on movement in specified areas. This would cover not only processions and meetings, but also, in relation to the threat of bombs and other attacks on property, the parking of vehicles and the approach to buildings of special vulnerability. As in the case of other emergency powers, however, provision should be made for an appeal to the emergency tribunal against any such order of restriction, and the tribunal should be granted full jurisdiction to rescind any order issued by the authorities.

In respect of civil disobedience, on the other hand, we have adopted the view that no derogation from the ordinary law of the land should be sought in emergency powers legislation. The basis of a campaign of civil disobedience, as we understand it, is that individuals or large numbers of persons are induced deliberately to break the law, whether by committing criminal offences or repudiating civil obligations, with a view to drawing attention to the alleged inequity of the law or in the case of mass action to rendering their enforcement impractical. Though in an extreme case such a campaign may be adopted with wide political objectives in view, it is generally linked to a broad acceptance of the authority of the courts and of any sanctions or penalties which may be imposed. Success is dependent on securing mass support either for any resulting political protest, or more directly on clogging the courts at an administrative level and so making the continued enforcement of the law impossible. In so far as these techniques are dependent on mass support and do not involve any deliberate rejection of the authority of the existing order by violent means, we feel that they should not be prohibited in any emergency powers legislation. Indeed the idea of prohibiting civil disobedience is something of a contradiction in terms. Legislative or administrative countermeasures may have to be taken in certain cases to prevent the disruption of essential services, but the merits of such measures can only be judged in the circumstances of the case. It would not be practical or desirable to attempt to provide in advance for matters of this kind in an emergency powers act designed to deal with violent subversion.

5. conclusion

These proposals could form the basis for emergency powers legislation for all or any of the jurisdictions in the British Isles. The question of the control over security in Northern Ireland is at present a matter of heated political controversy of a kind we have tried to avoid. However there are several general reasons for favouring the enactment of a new Emergency Powers Act to apply to the United Kingdom as a whole. First, in times of war or public emergency threatening the life of the nation, the whole nation is affected, even if the trouble is largely localised. In such circumstances it is desirable that the enacting and supervising authority should be in the central sovereign legislature, that is to say Parliament at Westminster. Secondly, it is desirable that authority for dealing with an emergency should not be fragmented and that confusions of the kind that have arisen in respect of the legality of some of the Army's operations in Northern Ireland should be avoided. Thirdly, it is desirable that standards and values in such a delicate area should be uniform throughout the United Kingdom. The *invocation* of the powers in a particular emergency may be localised, but the *principles* which govern such powers should be uniform. Fourthly, the United Kingdom is bound by international law to observe certain international standards. Finally, there is a need for a fundamental review of the law relating to emergency powers in the United Kingdom, in the light not only of the experience of Northern Ireland but also of experience in other Commonwealth countries since World War II. Recently no less an authority than Lord MacDermott, former Lord Chief Justice of Northern Ireland, said: "But law and order have recently been assailed in many ways the world over, and our malady may be yours tomorrow. What I would suggest is that, instead of meeting the problems I have mentioned piecemeal, it would be better and more effectual to enact an emergency code for the United Kingdom which would be applicable, as events warranted, to the whole or any part thereof and be operative only in times of crisis. The enactment of such a code would facilitate advance preparations and the implementation of our international obligations; and by its very existence it might go far to discourage subversion." That proposal should be given wholehearted support.

SUMMARY

The conclusions to this survey of emergency powers may be summarised:

1. There are serious defects in the form of the Special Powers Act as currently applied in Northern Ireland, and in particular in the absence of satisfactory controls and safeguards against the misuse and abuse of the powers granted to the security authorities. But the simple repeal of the Act would be equally unsatisfactory in that it would leave the security authorities to operate under vague and general common law powers which do not provide any greater measure of immediate protection or redress for the individual.

2. In place of the Special Powers Act a new Emergency Powers (Security) Act for the whole of the United Kingdom should therefore be adopted under which an emergency in any part of the United Kingdom might be dealt with. This new statute should contain provision for all the powers which the authorities may reasonably require to deal with an outbreak of violent subversion, but any derogation from the ordinary rights of the individual should be balanced by the provision of additional safeguards against abuse and of procedures for dealing with complaints and for the compensation of those who suffer loss or injury as a result.

3. The implementation of the emergency powers provided for in the new statute should be dependent on the declaration of a state of emergency in the area affected; this declaration should be ratified within a specified time by the Westminster Parliament; but if provision is made for the exercise of security powers by a regional legislature in Northern Ireland any declaration of emergency should also be reviewable by an independent judicial body.

4. The emergency powers provided for

in the statute should cover the power to stop and search any person, to require him to give an account of his movements, to detain any person for questioning on reasonable suspicion for a maximum period of 48 hours, and to search for and to seize any articles or evidence of unlawful activity.

5. The statute should make provision for emergency criminal offences covering any form of active involvement in violent subversive activity or active participation in any organisation whose objects or purposes include any form of violent subversion. The statute should make provision for any such organisation to be declared illegal, subject to a right of appeal to the courts for the review of any such declaration.

6. The statute should provide for the establishment of special criminal courts with jurisdiction to try any emergency offences provided for in the statute. The rules of procedure for such emergency courts should be provided for by regulation subject to parliamentary ratification.

7. The statute should provide for the establishment of a tribunal to hear complaints against the authorities for the misuse or abuse of any powers granted to them. The tribunal should have jurisdiction to award compensation to any person who suffers loss or injury as a result of any unreasonable action on the part of the authorities and in particular for any loss of income occasioned by the detention of any person. The rules of procedure before the tribunal should be designed to facilitate the speedy settlement of claims and to permit recovery and redress in a wider range of cases than is normally permissable under common law.

8. In view of its emotive significance both in Northern Ireland and in Britain as a whole the statute should *not* make advance provision for a power of internment without trial, but if any such power is subsequently adopted it should be accompanied with stringent prior and posterior safeguards.

9. The control of processions and other forms of non-violent protest should generally be left to be dealt with under permanent legislation, but provision should be included in an emergency powers statute for the making of orders restricting processions or meetings in specified times and places, and for restricting access to or movement in specified places, subject to the right of any person affected to appeal to the courts against any such order.

heads of legislation

The following is a very tentative outline for an Emergency Powers (Security) Act based on the above proposals.

Clause one: *Declaration of a state of emergency*: where it appears to the Secretary of State that as a result of violent subversion on the part of any person or persons a state of emergency exists in any part of the United Kingdom he may issue a proclamation to that effect, upon which any specified powers provided in this Act shall come into effect in the area specified in the proclamation.

Clause two: *Ratification*: unless the declaration of a state of emergency is ratified by affirmative resolution in both Houses of Parliament within two weeks of the proclamation it shall cease to have effect and shall not in any event have effect for longer than a period of six months unless further ratified.

Clause three: *Emergency offences*: it shall be an offence for any person (i) to engage in any violent subversive activity; (ii) to take an active part in the affairs of any organisation whose purposes include violent subversive activity of any kind or which has been declared to be illegal under the terms of this Act; (iii) to take part in the preparation, printing, publication or distribution of any publication or broadcast which contains any material inciting violent subversive activity or promoting any organisation which has been declared to be illegal under the terms of this Act.

Clause four: *Violent subversive activity*

for the purposes of this Act shall be deemed to cover any of the following activities undertaken with a view to securing whether directly or indirectly any political objective: (i) the use of fire-arms or explosives against any person or property; (ii) the infliction of malicious injury or damage on any person or property; (iii) the kidnapping of any person; (iv) the hijacking of any vehicle or vessel; (v) the forcible occupation of any premises; (vi) any other unlawful violent activity.

Clause five: *Illegal organisations*: any organisation which promotes or incites violent subversion in any form may be declared to be an illegal organisation for the purposes of this Act, provided that any person may make an application to the Court to determine whether the declaration of illegality is justified in all the circumstances.

Clause six: *Power to stop and search*: any person authorised under this Act may at any time stop and search any person, and may require him to reveal his name and address and to give an account of his movements at any time during the period of the emergency.

Clause seven: *Power to detain for questioning*: where an authorised person has reasonable cause to suspect that any person has not given a full and truthful answer to any question put to him under clause six he may detain him for further questioning for a period of up to 48 hours, and may for that purpose remove him to any place authorised for that purpose; the treatment of persons detained for questioning to be prescribed by regulations under this Act.

Clause eight: *Power to arrest*: all offences under this Act shall be deemed to be arrestable offences for the purposes of the Criminal Law Act 1967.

Clause nine: *Power of search and seizure*: any person authorised under this Act may without warrant search for and seize any article which he has reasonable grounds to believe is designed or intended for use in contravention of this Act, or which he has reasonable ground to believe constitutes admissable evidence of the commission of an offence under this Act.

Clause ten: *Emergency Criminal Courts*: provision for the constitution and jurisdiction of emergency courts to be provided for by regulation subject to ratification by Parliament.

Clause eleven: *Review Tribunal*: provision for the constitution and jurisdiction of a review tribunal to be provided for by regulation subject to ratification.

Clause twelve: *Miscellaneous powers*: The Secretary of State may at any time make an order restricting or prohibiting public processions or public meetings in any place, or restricting access to or movement in any place for a specified period, subject to the right of any person to make an application to the Court to determine whether the order was justified in all the circumstances.

fabian society

The Fabian Society exists to further socialist education and research. It is affiliated to the Labour Party, both nationally and locally, and embraces all shades of Socialist opinion within its ranks—left, right and centre.

Since 1884 the Fabian Society has enrolled thoughtful socialists who are prepared to discuss the essential questions of democratic socialism and relate them to practical plans for building socialism in a changing world.

Beyond this the Society has no collective policy. It puts forward no resolutions of a political character, but it is *not* an organisation of armchair socialists. Its members are active in their Labour Parties, Trade Unions and Co-operatives. They are representative of the labour movement, practical people concerned to study and discuss problems that matter.

The Society is organised nationally and locally. The national Society, directed by an elected Executive Committee, publishes pamphlets, and holds schools and conferences of many kinds. Local Societies—there are one hundred of them—are self governing and are lively centres of discussion and also undertake research.

Enquiries about membership should be sent to the General Secretary, Fabian Society, 11 Dartmouth Street, London, SW1H 9BN; telephone 01-930 3077.

the authors

The authors of this pamphlet were members of an informal group drawn from staff and students of the Faculty of Law of the Queen's University, Belfast. They had no official standing, and represented no one and the views expressed in this pamphlet are personal to themselves. The group was formed because it was felt that law students and law teachers might be able to contribute constructively to public discussion of some aspects of the Northern Ireland problem, and this pamphlet was produced primarily as a basis for such discussion. The group was drawn from people with widely differing views on the immediate situation in Northern Ireland, and from an even wider variety of backgrounds, but were united in their opposition to indiscriminate or reckless or unnecessary or unlawful use of violence either by the security forces or by anyone else. The group did not claim to be "apolitical" or impartial in their approach to the subject, but it did claim to represent a variety of political viewpoints and to share a respect for facts and for informed and reasoned analysis.

The members of the informal group were: R. L. Bentley (third year law student) J. O. Brady (fourth year law student) J. A. Caldwell (second year law student) T. B. Hadden (lecturer in law) G. Kerr (lecturer in law) N. Lambert (third year law student) L. J. Lysaght, Junior (visiting lecturer in law) J. C. McCrudden (second year law student) P. V. McGinley (third year law student) C. Palley (professor of law) W. L. Twining (professor of law, chairman of working party) M. P. Leneghan (third year law student, secretary of working party).

Cover design by Dick Leadbetter. Printed by Civic Press Limited (TU), Civic Street, Glasgow G4 9RH.

ISBN 7163 0416 3

recent fabian pamphlets

research series

268	M. Rendel and others	Equality for women	40p
291	David Stephen	Immigration and race relations	25p
292	John Gyford, Stephen Haseler	Social democracy: beyond revisionism	30p
294	John Southgate	Agricultural trade and the EEC	30p
297	Della Adam Nevitt	Fair deal for householders	25p
298	Jim Skinner	Collective bargaining and inequality	20p
299	S. F. Kissin	Communists: all revisionists now?	40p
300	Christopher Foster	Public enterprise	30p
301	Kees Maxey	From Rhodesia to Zimbabwe	45p
302	Arthur Gillette	Cuba's educational revolution	45p
303	Felicity Bolton, Jennie Laishley	Education for a multi-racial Britain	20p
304	Tessa Blackstone	First schools of the future	25p
305	O. Kahn-Freund, Bob Hepple	Laws against strikes	85p
306	Nicholas Deakin (ed)	Immigrants in Europe	40p
307	Paul Singh	Guyana: socialism in a plural society	25p

tracts

399	R. H. S. Crossman	Paying for the social services	20p
400	Anne Lapping (ed)	Community action	40p
404	Anthony Crosland	A social democratic Britain	15p
406	Giles Radice, J. O. N. Vickers	The industrial relations bill	15p
408	Eric Deakins	EEC problems for British agriculture	25p
409	Wayland Kennet and others	Sovereignty and multinational companies	30p
410	Anthony Crosland	Towards a Labour housing policy	20p
411	Dennis Marsden	Politicians, equality and comprehensives	30p
412	Jeremy Bray	The politics of the environment	25p
413	Michael Stewart	Labour and the economy: a socialist strategy	35p
414	ten Fabian task forces	Towards a radical agenda: comments on Labour's programme	50p

young fabian pamphlets

17	Colin Crouch (ed)	Students today	30p
22	M. Blades, D. Scott	What price Northern Ireland?	20p
24	Elizabeth Durkin	Hostels for the mentally disordered	15p
27	Isla Calder	Our children's teachers	30p
28	Colin Crouch, Stephen Mennell	The universities: pressures and prospects	45p
29	Russell Lansbury	Swedish social democracy	25p
30	James Bellini	British entry: Labour's nemesis	25p
31	James Goudie	Councils and the Housing Finance Act	30p

books

R. H. S. Cr	£1.75
Margaret C	£0.75
Brian Abel-	£0.60
B. Lapping	£1.25
Peter Town	£0.75
Peter Town	£0.90
George Cu	£3.00
P. Townsen	£2.20